FAIRLEY

BARKER
FAIRLEY
PORTRAITS

With a text by the Artist
Edited with an Introduction by
Gary Michael Dault

🔷 Methuen

Toronto   New York   London   Sydney   Auckland

Canadian Cataloguing in Publication Data
Fairley, Barker, 1887-
Barker Fairley portraits

Bibliography: p.
ISBN 0-458-95150-1 (bound). — ISBN 0-458-95160-9 (gallery)

1. Fairley, Barker, 1887-   I. Title.

ND249.F34A4 1981   759.11   C81-095002-2

Printed and bound in Canada

1 2 3 4 5   81   86 85 84 83 82

For Bill and Burt

This book is dedicated to Bill and Burt — that is to say, to Bill Shelden and Burt Richardson, who as longtime friends of the artist and supporters of his work both took it upon themselves to publish an edition of Barker Fairley's poems and then to suggest that there ought to be a volume of his portraits. I hope this book is something like the book they would have made.

G.M.D.

· INTRODUCTION ·

To be painted by Barker Fairley is to be subjected to the kind of scrutiny you never forget. I had known Barker for six years, and for six years I had put it off. It was getting to the point, however, where to go on refusing was going to look rude. And so, one sunny morning last May, I knocked on the door of the handsome old house on Willcocks Avenue at precisely ten o'clock — as every sitter had to (Barker has always been precise about the ten o'clock start) — and climbed the stairs to the bright little studio on the second floor.

He began straightaway. He put me in a fine, burnished, old captain's chair in the middle of the studio and retired to his easel over by the window. He slipped on the smock decorated with the fallout from a hundred earlier portraits, donned a tiny and, I thought, rather unfairly keen and hawkish pair of spectacles, and set resolutely to work. "You may talk to me if you wish," he told me, "though I may not say much in reply." "What do you want me to do?" I asked, feeling foolish about so virginal a question, especially after having written about his painting a number of times before and having, until now, felt reasonably familiar with it. "The best thing would be to sit still," he suggested and then, as further help for the novice sitter, "Why don't you look over my shoulder and out the window? Fix your eyes on some feature of the house across the street and look at that." I did. Wholeheartedly. And with what I fervently hoped was an enormous amount of the right kind of portrait-like raptness and middle-distance remoteness in my eyes.

First he drew an outline in charcoal. He made a lot of quick jabbings and arcings at the canvas, a sort of claiming of me in line that made me both queasy and exhilarated. I wanted to come around and see the finished drawing. There aren't a lot of Barker Fairley drawings around, after all, and here was a perfectly good one about six feet away. "Don't move," he snapped. I decided not to.

It was quite a long time before I shifted my eyes from the brick chimney across the way and risked a glance at what he was doing. Mostly he was looking at me. He would look for a long time, then plunge his brush into the little puddle of bright oil paint on the table next to him, thrust the pigment onto the canvas, and scratch and scumble it around. It sounded like somebody walking on dry leaves. Sometimes, when he would change colours, he would hold the first brush in his mouth while painting with the second. I remember glancing at him at one point and finding his lips had turned royal blue.

There came a point at which he felt he no longer needed me in front of him. "You're free to get up and move around," he told me, "if you want to." I didn't, particularly, and so I stayed in the captain's chair, watching his bright vivacious eyes, intent now on the blooming image in front of him, an image that seemed to have taken on a life of its own. The only sound in the room was the insistent rasp of the brush.

He finished the picture by noon. Most of Barker's portraits are made in two hours from ten until noon. Barker's wife Nan came into the studio just as he was putting his brushes aside. "Barker," she said excitedly, "you really are something of a shaman."

"Well, anyhow," he replied with a happy smile, "let's all of us have a glass of beer."

"I know I'm not doing professional portraits," Barker told me afterwards, "and I'm not after a likeness merely. I've often failed miserably to get a likeness — at least the first time. What I'm seeking is an *aspect* of the face. Something by which a face becomes humane and *reflects* on humanity. When it does happen that way, it happens because of the visual freedom I give myself."

The visual freedom he gives himself would be radical in any serious artist. It is all the more extraordinary in Barker Fairley because of the way his career as a painter began and the way it has developed.

Barker Fairley is now in his ninety-fifth year. He was born in Yorkshire, in a little coal-mining town called Barnsley, in May of 1887. His ancestors on his father's side were sea-faring men, for the most part, though his father was, atypical for the family, a schoolmaster. One of the Fairley men of each generation has borne the Christian name Barker. "It means somebody whose job it was to strip the bark off trees," Barker once told me. "It's a name I dislike intensely."

A bookish but not unrobust boy, the young Barker Fairley played soccer and worked at his studies — both with considerable diligence. He did not draw or paint. "I didn't paint a line until I was forty-four years old," Barker said. "I was convinced I couldn't draw. I'd never made a drawing in my life before middle age." "Didn't you make drawings as a child?" I once asked him. "I thought *all* children made drawings." "As a boy at school, I shaded cones and cylinders with a stub of charcoal," he replied, the distaste of it still vivid in his memory — and alive in his face. "Oh, it was miserable. The master once wrote my parents, 'This boy needs special attention.' I knew that meant I *wasn't* an artist."

What he was, however, was a scholar — at least in embryo. The young Fairley worked sufficiently hard to win a county scholarship to the University of Leeds where he read Modern Languages. He was graduated with first class honours in both French and German. From Leeds, he became an instructor at Jena where, for three pastoral years that, to hear Barker speak of them, sound like scenes from *The Student Prince*, he taught and, at the same time, earned his Ph.D.

He came to Canada in 1910 to teach at what was then just barely the University of Alberta. The University was at that time occupying the upper floor of the Strathcona Collegiate Institute in Edmonton. The young scholar had a great deal of time to wander under the prairie sky and drink up great draughts of what he would later refer to as "the primary Canadian fact — our geography." It was in Edmonton that he married Margaret Keeling (in 1914), a brilliant young literature student who had been refused a degree at Oxford because she was a woman but was offered not only a teaching post at the new University of Alberta, but was also made the University's Dean of Women (a nice irony, when you think about it for a moment) — again, not an exhausting job when you consider the number of women enrolled at the time. Both Margaret and Barker taught. And they read. Indeed, they seem to have read everything in Edmonton at the time. Eventually, they had five children. Only two are still living. Margaret herself died in 1967. One of Barker's portraits of her is reproduced here (page 11).

In 1915 Barker Fairley accepted the post of Professor of German Literature at the University of Toronto. "When I first came to Toronto it was a dreary, unimaginative city," Barker remembers, "and yet my intellectual life really began here. It was in Toronto that I came to intellectual maturity."

In Toronto he met J.E.H. ("Jimmie") MacDonald, A.Y. Jackson, Fred Varley, and the other painters of the then controversial Group of Seven. Barker didn't paint with them, but he watched them paint and travelled with them, and carried on endless discussions with them about making pictures. He became, in fact, the first real champion, defender, and critic the Group had.

Barker Fairley's founding of *The Canadian Forum* in 1920 also had a bearing on both the critical fortunes of the Group and on his own visual education. It was not long after his arrival at the University of Toronto that the young Professor Fairley found himself acting as faculty advisor to a clutch of enthusiastic students who were putting together a cheeky little student paper called *The Rebel*. Like clutches of enthusiastic students everywhere, the begettors of *The Rebel* eventually ran out of steam and the paper languished. It was Barker's idea to take it beyond the campus. Indeed, he had big plans for it. He remembers his exact words at the time: "Let's go to the country with it!" And so *The Canadian Forum* was born.

The *Forum* was of major importance to Barker's painter friends, first because he got them to contribute drawings, woodcuts and linocuts to decorate the magazine's handsome, restrained pages; and second because he saw to it that the *Forum* provided a measured and intelligent countervoice to the shrieks of agony and disbelief then blistering the popular press whenever the Group exhibited their paintings. Both Barker and Margaret held editorial positions on the new magazine. And it was in the pages of *The Canadian Forum* that Barker wrote his first art criticism.

Barker Fairley is a formidably intellectual man, but his art criticism was never heavily or exhaustively analytical. Rather, he proceeded from painting to painting, allowing himself the pleasure of the full intuitive play of a highly symbolic and sometimes puckishly metaphorical imagination over every work he examined. Pictures seemed to speak to him in ways that were uncrackably lyrical and in ways that were deeper than discursive language. When Barker wrote about a painting he wrote a prose that attempted to match the sensuousness of the picture in front of him.

He took himself seriously as a critic and was never especially easy on his friends in the Group. He was their champion, yes. But he could also be their most demanding and constructive commentator. It was as early as the *Forum* for June 1921, for example, that he took a long, rather unhappy look at Lawren Harris's "Island — MacCallum Lake" and found it troubling — and wanting. The drawing, the handling of the paint and the painter's use of colour seemed to be flying apart in different directions: "It would seem as if head, heart and hand had worked in ignorance of one another," Barker wrote. "Human nature cannot cope with dreams that are more solid than reality or with ghost stories that are as boisterous as trumpets. The blood refuses to freeze and to palpitate at one and the same time. Mr. Harris offers an incongruous thing, an oxymoron, a bitter-sweet, a choke-cherry." Harris seemed to Barker to have fallen a victim to "blind partitions within his mind which keep it from fusing." "The three gray sisters in the classical myth," he wrote, "had one eye between them which they passed from one to the other. When the one could see, the other two were temporarily blind. The eye often got lost and suffered as an instrument from irregular use. There is perhaps a special meaning for Mr. Harris in this little legend."

Varley, on the other hand, was as firm and whole as Harris was divided. It was in Varley that Barker Fairley discovered "great formal achievement without the slightest abatement of reality" and "strong emotion under perfect control" (both phrases, by the way, admirable descriptions of the paintings that Barker would later make for himself). For Varley, art will not boil down to a set of precepts. Varley's four famous war canvases approached greatness because of their irreducibility: "The only other artists who attempted as much had recourse to formula. Paul Nash satirized war by making geometry of it. Mr. Varley, by greater force of temperament, was able to dispense with such devices and simply digest the whole concern."

Opposed all his life to art theory in place of a more corporeal and sensuously unified experience of art, the young critic had already in the first issue of the *Forum* (October 1920) come out against theory as one of the experiences of the mind he would later refer to as "sandpaperings of the human spirit." "Theory is not enough to produce great art," he wrote. "It is only one side of the story and the other side is some objective world in which the theory can lose itself, dissolve itself. Call it what you will. The place for theory in the finished work is that of the skylark that loses itself in the blue, heard but not seen, forgotten yet flooding the air with melody. In many . . . modern paintings the theory sits on the fence and croaks." Too much theory and a work of art tips out of that delicate balance that makes it humanly accessible and invigorating. When that happens, the work falls into time and becomes "eccentric" — or, as Barker often puts it, "odd." When philosophies and human societies become jumbled and incoherent, "the artist cannot immerse himself in them. And so he feels his way from oddity to oddity, unloading hell behind him step by step." A work of art that is "odd" finds itself beached high upon the decade of its conception where, passed by the great tradition of the humanly usable, it dwindles into a curiosity for historians.

With his own painting still a few years ahead of him, it happened that in 1922, when he was thirty-five, Barker nevertheless started to produce highly personal works of primary art in the form of a whole series of neatly turned and entirely unbidden poems. He won't talk about what it was that opened the floodgates through which these deft and frequently moving little lyrics tumbled. Whatever it was ("It was something in my life that wouldn't interest anybody else and which you wouldn't believe even if I told you," he once explained to me), the poems came to him fully made, ready to be written out. "The fact is that I was a poet for one year and *not* a poet for the other ninety-three," Barker reminded me recently. The poems, like the paintings he would eventually make, are unfailingly lean and sinewy. Sometimes when they are gay or high-spirited, satirical or bittersweet, they sound a bit Georgian, a bit A.E. Housman. More often, they have a muscular, nugget-like solidity that lends them a special compression and eloquence which is unlike poetry by anyone else. The poem that perhaps best demonstrates this *multum-in-parvo* crystallization of sound and meaning is the poem I have heard Barker say he would like to see preserved and perhaps (he is a bit wistful about this) remembered. The poem is called "The Rock."

No mortal mother made me
To feel the warm blood flow,
The years have not betrayed me
To hunger and to know.

A wiser mother made me;
From searings and from shock
The cooling years have stayed me.
I am the rock.

The rock is, of course, the Precambrian shield. It is also, surely, a symbol for the poet of the same kind of irreducible experience that ought to infuse and order all significant works of the human spirit, works that lie beyond style and beyond theory, works that the years, as it were, cannot betray.

It ought to be remembered, by the way, that all of this hobnobbing with painters, writing of art criticism and the composing of poetry was going on as a sort of sharp brass flourishing over and above a bass continuum of university teaching and scholarly writing. Barker wrote his first book in 1926. It was a study of the great English poet and prose master Charles M. Doughty, whose epic poem about the origins of English society, "The Dawn in Britain," and his extravagantly rich and lustrous account of his life among the Arabian peoples in the 1870s, "Travels in Arabia Deserta," Barker believes to be the two inexplicably neglected masterworks of English literature. The book was written in a white heat upon Barker's learning of Doughty's death in 1926. He sat down and wrote a chapter a week for ten weeks. The book was published by Jonathan Cape in 1927.

Although he has published books about Heinrich Heine and the German novelist William Raabe, it is as a student of the life and works of Goethe that Barker Fairley is best known. He has written three books about Goethe — whom he regards as the greatest figure in European literature since Shakespeare — at least one of which, his *A Study of Goethe* published by the Clarendon Press in 1947, has never been surpassed in its field and is today an acknowledged classic of Goethe criticism. In 1970 the University of Toronto Press published Barker's prose translation of Goethe's *Faust*. It is regarded by many scholars of German literature as the best translation of Faust ever made.

Surrounded on all sides by important artist friends, art talk, and art writing — and with his teaching career humming along successfully (punctuated at a stately and academically appropriate rhythm by the publication of the books that were making him famous), it would seem almost inevitable that Barker should have begun to paint his own pictures. As it turned out, it wasn't inevitable at all. "My friends in the Group of Seven never said, 'Why don't you paint instead of talking about it?'" Barker complained a few months ago. "One of them *should* have said that, but nobody did," he told me. "Arthur Lismer lent me his studio one winter when he was away . . . that was friendly. Fred Varley once pointed to a rather suicidal-looking head of a woman I made after I had started to paint and said to me, 'You can't *do* that!' That's all he said. 'You can't *do* that!' He also said my pictures were very intense . . . but that's all."

How, then, did Barker Fairley ever get to be a painter in his own right? The way Barker tells it, it happened because in 1931, when he was forty-four years old, he was finally *made* to paint by a colleague at the University of Toronto, poet and painter Robert Finch. "Robert wanted to see what I thought about *his* paintings," Barker explained, "and after we'd talked awhile, he suggested that I take up painting as well." He went even further. "I remember telling Margaret," Barker recalled, "that Robert had said he would be around for me on Sunday with water colours and paper and that we would go out sketching together — and that I said I hoped it would rain so I shouldn't have to go." As it turned out it did not rain and the two friends went out in search of pictures. "Robert denies this whole story," Barker says. "But it's entirely true. All of it!"

One of the paintings he made on that historically significant day hangs in the Fairley living room right now. It is a tiny watercolour painting of an apple orchard in blossom, the thin golden light of the sun veiling down over the bright pink of the apple boughs. It is a superb painting and, considering the conditions under which it was made, astonishingly assured. "I hadn't to *acquire* any sort of painting *style,* you see," Barker told me. "I had a style immediately — I found myself already grown up in it. The way I paint now is not very different from the way I painted that apple orchard." In a sense, the paintings came almost the way the poems had, unforced, unbidden — as lyrical shots in the dark, with no accompanying theory to weigh them down.

The great appeal of a Barker Fairley painting is its freshness, its look of the artist's having newly understood something or having seen something for the first time. Every landscape, every portrait Barker makes is an opportunity to play once again the Adamic game of *naming* — as if he and all of us too were for a moment back in the garden where everything had to be invented all over. A Fairley orchard is pink with the light that the trees themselves give off — if only we could see that delicately. A lake in a Fairley landscape is blue and stridently *horizontal* in the way that a child's lake is, or the way a lake would be if you were trying to describe it to somebody who had never seen one. For most of us a tree is only a tree. For Barker — in his paintings, at least — a tree is a living twist of energy that holds the sky up off the surface of the earth. The eyes in a Fairley portrait are vivid jellies through which the life of the human spirit flashes like water glimpsed through a forest.

Barker's career as a painter did not, however, progress smoothly from 1931 to the present, its incandescent beginnings notwithstanding. In 1932 he accepted an offer to become head of the German department at the University of Manchester. "I hated to leave Canada," Barker told me, "but it was too important a position to refuse. The funny thing is that I thought Margaret wanted me to take it, and she thought I wanted to take it. I didn't find out until much later that neither of us wanted to go. It was the only time I think we ever had such a misunderstanding. Neither of us really wanted to leave Canada, you see."

Barker painted in Manchester — but not much. His "Head," (Jewish Girl) 1933, was painted there (page 21) along with a few other portraits — his first attempts at the genre. And he did some gloomy Manchester industry-scapes, all satanic mills and sad, depleted workers in the midst of what was by then world-wide depression. In three years he was back in Canada.

Partly because of his new duties as head of the German department at the University of Toronto, and partly, perhaps, because of the decisive break from the painting he had been doing effected by his sojourn in Manchester, Barker found it difficult upon his return to Canada to take up his painting where he had left it three years before. I remember his telling me about his rage at not any longer being able to paint his beloved Georgian Bay, at "failing utterly" at it, and in something like despair doing the best he could to capture the landscape in quick rough pencil sketches. He wrote in the preface to a collection of these sketches published by the University of Toronto Press in 1957, ". . . the shift from grey-green Derbyshire to the sparkle of a Georgian Bay summer was too much for me." In 1940 Barker and a group of friends (including painters John Hall and Aba Bayefsky) rented a studio at 22 Hayden Street in Toronto where they could attend to the painting of the figure. A few rather academic pictures later, Barker Fairley put away his paints and brushes and gave up painting entirely for almost ten years.

It was at a resort in Northern Ontario called Jackknife Lodge owned by painter Vincent Thomas (page 61) that Barker was once again, in 1953, pushed into painting — this time by Thomas and by his own son-in-law John Hall (page 57). He's been painting steadily ever since — and painting with an accelerating clarity and economy of means that almost every week, even now in his ninety-fifth year, results in something extraordinary.

Barker Fairley's landscapes are in great demand just now. Understandably. The leanness and severity of their composition is radical and the radiant colour that flows from each of them is irresistible. But to Barker it is the portrait that is important. "There is a well-developed landscape tradition in Canada," Barker points out, "but there is really no similar tradition within the art of the human figure. Varley did some things — very fine things too — but really, there isn't much. Why this should be is puzzling." "Maybe," he once suggested to me, "this is still a young country. Maybe it just hasn't got around to portraits yet." Perhaps it is just that our vastnesses preclude the intimacies of portraiture. Maybe we map ourselves beyond the smaller but more powerful topologies of the personal. Whatever the reason, Barker Fairley deplores our national neglect of the humanistic rewards that lie hidden within an art of each other.

"I know I'm not doing professional portraits," Barker had told me, and I knew what he meant. Some of them are, in fact, crude — in a way that happens only when great energy is trapped within a format that will no longer easily contain it. The painterly storms raging through Barker's portrait of his friend Christopher Grieve (page 51), for example, and the deep slicings of white and black and blue by which the artist has carved Hugh Garner (page 67) out of what might have been a slag-heap of raw blue pigment, are part of an expressionist explosion that either distresses the people who look at these pictures or, on the other hand, forces them to see and to feel — indeed, almost to re-enact — the painter's attempt to get down in paint the rich, sometimes joyful, sometimes painful, always demanding world of another human being.

Barker's portraits often have the kind of internal emotional force that distresses even the artist himself — as if he were the transformer through which the sitter's vital meanings were suddenly available. Barker's portrait of his friend Emil Gartner (page 47) upset him when he was painting it and continues to disturb him whenever he looks at it. "He had terrible anguish in his face," Barker told me, "and when I painted him, I struck through him to the terrifying nomadic world of his ancestors. I felt that somehow I was in the *desert* with his grandfather. Even now, whenever I hear the music from Handel's *Judas Maccabaeus* that Emil once conducted, whenever I hear 'Sound the alarm, your silver trumpets sound,' I think of him *there* . . . I think of him *deep in the desert!*" Everything in this remarkable portrait is alive. Even the subject's shirt seems to writhe. The eyes are like a wolf's.

Nor is Barker less disturbing in what are ostensibly meditative moods. His delicate and upsetting portrait of the little lost Brigitte (page 77), for example, is painted in such a way that Brigitte is scarcely there in the picture at all. Her face is made up of the same airless chalkiness as the background. Her hair is almost the same colour as her coat — as if she were herself no more substantial than what she puts on. The collar of her coat is thin and meagre. She is utterly unprotected. She dwindles to nothing at all as you look at her.

Not all of Barker's portraits, of course, are tossed and troubled. His apple-cheeked study of his grandson Dick Schabas (page 85) is the best and most concentrated essay on quintessential boyhood I've ever seen. His wine-dark and plum-coloured portrait of E.J. Pratt (page 65) is wonderfully robust and hearty. His Donald Creighton (page 3) is a portrait of a curmudgeon — and suffers fools no more gladly than its sitter would have. His Robertson Davies (page 71) is vertical (lofty, even), hieratic, icon-like. His Northrop Frye (page 49), gentle, puckish and wise.

In portrait after portrait, there is a running through of all the emotions we have to show; fifty portraits together is like an emotional rainbow, a morality play stretching silently throughout the fifty years in which Barker Fairley has been making pictures.

On the last page of his text for this book, Barker remembers his conversations with his friend and one-time colleague Laura Hofrichter about the "human meaning" locked within his pictures, about the outlook on life that the paintings reveal. I now think that outlook on life has something intimately to do with a great humanist's restless search for more and more that is the stuff of which humanity is made. Sometimes I feel that Barker Fairley has been trying feverishly to paint the entire family of man — men, women, children, young people, old people. Does he not care about individual likenesses, about fidelity to the geography of each of his sitters? At the time he does. Ultimately he probably does not. Not when compared to the moving generalities that make the shape of the human presence the only study that can now nourish him. One of the poems he wrote in 1922 is even more true today:

> Hungry I was
> And fed on fullness,
> Yet life was such
> I knew but dullness.
>
> Older I am
> And yet am younger;
> My life is full,
> I feed on hunger.

Barker and I were driving somewhere a few months ago, and while we were sitting at a stoplight he began to recite some German poetry. Goethe, I imagined. I wasn't sure.

> "Was willst du, dass von deiner Gesinnung
>   man dir nach ins Ewige sende?"
> "Er gehörte zu keiner Innung,
>   Blieb Liebhaber bis ans Ende."

"What's that?" I asked him. "Goethe," he answered. "An epigram he wrote in his mid-eighties." "What is he saying?" I asked. "Will you settle for a very free translation of my own?" he asked me. "Of course," I said.

> "What do you want them to say about you
>   when you've gone?"
> "Say I never toed a line,
>   I went my own sweet way to the last."

GARY MICHAEL DAULT

• THE PORTRAITS •

Donald Creighton

Starting off with Donald Creighton, am I? Well, why not? I chose him not solely or even chiefly because he is our leading historian and a writer of great prose in a country which has all too little, but because his face simply called to be painted, and forces itself on me now.

Here then is Donald at his severest, or not far from it. For myself I would rather make a severe start than a soft one, if I had to choose. And few will question its appropriateness in presenting him of all people, a man who ruthlessly spoke his mind on all occasions. So let him speak to you now on the page facing you.

Those observers who at first glance shrink from so powerful a countenance are apt to glance nervously over his shoulder — as I frequently observe — and ask me about the background, jumping, I won't say from the sublime to the ridiculous, but at any rate, from the more uncomfortable to the less. Well, the background came from a thin trickle of raw umber — my indispensable colour — that I let run down over the darkened off-white board the day before, little suspecting that I should leave so much of it untouched in the finished work. Actually, all I painted, after making the brush-drawing, was the head and one hand. The thing suddenly seemed to me finished, in the sense that anything I added would detract from the force it now had. So here it is in its near monochrome and its directness.

Donald Creighton, 1969
76 cm x 101.6 cm (30" x 40")
Oil on masonite
Collection: Mr. and Mrs. Ernest DuVernet

3

W.J. Alexander

This is the Alexander of the well-attended Alexander lectures, given annually in his honour at Hart House. He was very kind to me on my coming to Toronto in 1915, and we became great friends in spite of the difference in our ages. I recall him jokingly reminding me that he was born in the same year as my father in 1856.

If I remember rightly, I painted Alexander three times soon after meeting him again on my return to Toronto, say in 1936 or 1937. The portrait here shown is the last and the smallest and the best of the three. I have always treasured it and am confident that it represents him reasonably well. It may be that the amount of blue I used was not quite what his sobriety called for. But it doesn't hurt him, and having drifted into using it freely, I let it stand. He never uttered a syllable by way of comment on my work. But this silence on his part may not have meant disapproval so much as lack of interest. My experience with intellectuals is that scientists as a whole are much closer to painting and the visual arts than men of letters. Thus both Banting and Best were painters in their spare time. I could elaborate this observation abundantly out of my own experience over more than half a century.

Let me tell an amusing item of memory. All I remember of the first walk we had together. It was this. I caught sight of an unfamiliar shrub and said, "What's that?" and he said, "That's sumach." I had never seen it before or heard the unfamiliar word pronounced, and the surprise it gave me has stayed with me ever since.

W.J. Alexander, 1936
27.9 cm x 33 cm (11" x 13")
Oil on canvas
Private Collection

Esther Lutzky

Esther Lutzky was a dressmaker who lived for years on Robert Street, not far from my home on Willcocks Avenue. I haven't seen her about for a long time, and can't help wondering whether she has just moved locally to another address or whether she has gone on the longest journey of all. She was known to be a good dressmaker, but I knew better what she excelled in — she was the ideal sitter for a portrait. Exactly what the qualifications are for that distinction I don't know. But she had them. She knew just what was required of her. Being an expert dressmaker, she knew what to wear, and if she sat again she knew what to wear the next time. Once seated, she was completely self-forgetful, yet never weary or absent-minded or restless. I doubt if she was ever called beautiful, but she had that in her face that was better than beauty, a sense of the long tradition she was descended from, the tradition of people who worked, call it a folk-tradition, something that set her free from any impulse to compose herself or strike a gesture. She just relaxed naturally and no more was needed. I have had a lot of sitters and she was the best.

She came back into my mind one day not long ago when I had dinner at the house of Ben and Ricky Schachter. The Schachters have an unusual collection of pictures evidently chosen with care. I looked around and wished I was one of the company on their walls, when lo and behold there round the corner was Esther Lutzky. The name slowly shaped itself, and after this came the realization that it was I who had painted her. But not before I had first experienced the picture independently of myself and been able to contemplate it for a few seconds as if someone else had done it. I had no doubt about including her in my choice of fifty. So here she is. She chose herself.

Esther Lutzky, 1965
39.4 cm x 50.8 cm (15½" x 20")
Oil on masonite
Collection: Mr. and Mrs. Ben Schachter

Norman Endicott

There seems to be no other way of identifying my portraits than by identifying the sitter. In this case there was a dilemma because Norman disliked what I did with him and I promised him not to exhibit it, adding, however, that I wasn't going to destroy it either. We left it at that, and now that he is gone I feel free to let it be seen in its own right. No one has questioned its independent value. I certainly came by it honestly, never having had anything but complete friendliness toward him throughout the many years we were colleagues at University College, University of Toronto.

How it turned out the way it did I am at a loss to say. To those two or three who have asked me why I put that halo behind him, I replied that I had never seen a halo that went down behind the back of the neck. It simply came into my head as an extension of the rounded form of the rest. Ought I to have taken it out? It is one of my early things, painted in Arthur Lismer's studio on Bedford Road, which he gave me the use of the year he was away in England, somewhere around 1940 and certainly not before 1937. A happy memory for me.

Norman Endicott, 1938
30.5 cm x 45.7 cm (12" x 18")
Oil on canvas
Private Collection

Margaret Fairley

When you look back on a fifty-years' marriage, you prefer to be excused from talking about it. So I excuse myself.

But I can say a word about my two portraits. The one reproduced here was done, I remember, soon after 1936, when I was sharing a studio on McCaul Street with Gordon Webber. Margaret was unwilling to sit for long and soon jumped up and left me with little more than a drawing. I appreciated her independence as indicating a better attitude to a husband than that of the adoring wife which I now and then saw other men suffering from. This didn't help me to finish the picture, but it explains why it is so highly stylized and idealized. Some of us think it reveals her more truly, more deeply, than the much later one I did, which by contrast was done at her request. A good one, too. I remember her saying, "You don't need to destroy this one," which, I am sure, was not intended to convey a rejection of the first.

And now back to my silence.

Margaret Fairley, 1937
28.6 cm x 39.4 cm (11¼" x 15½")
Oil on wood panel
Collection: Mr. and Mrs. Ezra Schabas

Earle Birney

I knew Earle Birney best when he was an inconspicuous member of the English department in University College. It wasn't till he gave a public lecture on Chaucer that I realized he *was* somebody. I wonder if he remembers that lecture or if he kept a copy of it? It was somewhat later that he published "David" and made himself known as a poet.

I half-remember that he had thoughts of buying my portrait of him but desisted because someone had stolen his purse in the residence. Does he recall this? Or am I wrong? My painting indicates a twist in his right cheek. He told me his father had it.

Earle Birney, 1957
44.5 cm x 54.6 cm (17½" x 21½")
Oil on masonite
Collection: Mr. and Mrs. Ernest DuVernet

13

Jane Jacobs

Jane Jacobs came to live in Canada some ten years ago and evidently prefers to live a quiet life here. But I couldn't think of leaving her out of my little portrait gallery. And consequently I have to say a word about her. I shall try to be as cool about it as I can.

In her native country she is a prominent figure. According to an article on her in *New York Magazine* (February 1978) she is America's foremost critic of urban planning. Her first book, *The Death and Life of Great American Cities*, (1961), has perceptibly, dramatically, permanently, changed our views on this subject — something the like of which can rarely be said of any book on any region of society. So the article tells us. Whether Toronto too has profited by her thinking, without our knowing it, is possible enough. But we are not yet out of the woods, and I for one am glad indeed that she is in our midst.

As for my portrait, I can't help saying of her personally much what others have said of her writings: she is one of a few, a very few, who stand out in my mind as better, grander than the rest of us. I find in her a largeness, a generosity of spirit that singles her out among mankind. It simply oozes out of her, whether she likes it or not. When actually painting her I wasn't thinking about this. I always work visually and the sitter's personality looks after itself, as it can be trusted to do.

Jane Jacobs, 1973
40.6 cm x 50.8 cm (16" x 20")
Oil on masonite
Private Collection

15

Claude Bissell

In preparing this book some of the happier moments come when I get the opportunity to celebrate an old friend. As now with Claude Bissell. My memory doesn't improve with age. But I can definitely go back to what must be the later thirties when Claude, a lecturer in English at University College, was working on Samuel Butler, the later one, and I was able to give him a German study of that author, which he welcomed.

If I have made him look severer than one expects, I don't want to make a change. When people tell me I don't paint smiling faces I say, "Do you think of yourself as smiling?" and they always say "no." Anyway you are free to forget about Simcoe Hall and picture Claude at his summer place on Cape Breton, which he is proud of. Driving through that country some years ago, I tried to find it and failed. Too bad, because I don't expect to be over that way again.

Claude Bissell, 1975
76.2 cm x 101.6 cm (30" x 40")
Oil on masonite
Private Collection

Edgar Simon

This of Edgar Simon is one of the very few portraits I painted along with others. I know of two more of him done at the same time. The date is 1940 or soon after.

A group of us had rented the upper floor of a small warehouse on Hayden Street in Toronto in 1940. We had the use of the big room all the time, but we met regularly once a week to work on a common subject. Usually it was a chosen theme for which we did our own posing. This plan worked wonderfully well. I remember an evening with two men shooting craps, another of chess-players, and one of an accidental death, showing the body and two mourners.

Now and then we did a portrait, and Edgar came one evening and sat for us. His sister, Ellen Simon, was one of the gang. He was, at that time, at college, and has ever since worked at the Canadian Press. We are old friends who never meet. But this work brought us happily together again. He reminded me that he had been one of my students.

Edgar Simon, c. 1940
63.5 cm x 76.2 cm (25" x 30")
Oil on masonite
Private Collection

Jewish Girl

Nothing seems to please people more, when they look at my work, than to tell me I have changed in style. The truth of it is that there has been no change to speak of. Or, at most, a refinement. My style was there the day I started and has stayed with me right along. Witness this "Jewish Girl," which shows my characteristic strong lines and flat areas and was painted within little more than a year of my starting to paint at all and within a month or so of my starting to do portraits, most of half a century ago. This is, I believe, the only portrait chosen for this volume that was not painted in Canada.

Head, 1933
(Jewish Girl)
27.9 cm x 33 cm (11" x 13")
Oil on canvas
Collection: Mr. and Mrs. John Sommer

Joe Wallace

Joe Wallace I have always thought of as Canada's communist poet, if Canada ever wanted one. His collected verses are to be published soon, and we might as well have a look at them. After all, we act Brecht's plays without question, so why not read what Joe has to say? Not that he was a great genius, but he stood for something, which is not a bad thing in a poet, and he was a native Canadian.

There is one little poem of his that I have never been able to get out of my mind. Nor will you get it out of yours once you know it. So pause before you read on. He was a prisoner at Petawawa for a while in 1941 in solitary confinement and he wrote:

> My prison window is not large,
> Five inches high, six inches wide,
> Perhaps seven.
> Yet it is large enough to show
> The whole unfettered to and fro
> Of heaven. How high, how wide, is heaven?
> Five inches high, six inches wide,
> Perhaps seven.

Of my portrait of Joe, someone once said that it made him look demonic. And at another time someone else said it made him look like Mephistopheles. There must be some truth in these comments, though I had no such thoughts myself. So let them stand. And remember that a great poet makes God in heaven say somewhere that the devil too has good in him, because he stirs people up and so serves a creative purpose in spite of himself. Or words to that effect. And anyway Joe Wallace is safely dead now.

Joe Wallace, 1957
35.6 cm x 38.1 cm (14" x 15")
Oil on masonite
Private Collection

Bena Schuster

At the point of completing this portrait of Bena, I realized how full it was of sex, never having had my attention drawn so definitely that way before in all my painting. This gave me an added reason for including it, as extending my range. When I told her what I was going to say, she quietly assented. I suspect her of being a wise woman.

Bena Schuster, 1973
35 cm x 50.2 cm (13¾" x 19¾")
Oil on masonite
Collection: Bena Schuster

Carl Schaefer

It isn't easy for me to show a portrait of Carl Schaefer when I think of the masterly portrait Charles Comfort did of him. But that was long ago and he was young then. There may be some justification. Besides, I have other excuses, quite apart from the fact that Carl is a wonderful subject whom no one who paints faces could resist.

He and I have had a long-standing affiliation. His first appearance as an artist, if I am not mistaken, was with a linocut in *The Canadian Forum* in the nineteen-twenties when I was in on it and Thoreau MacDonald was art editor and doing most of the illustrations himself. This means that Carl knew the MacDonalds, father and son, as I did. And who that knew them together could ever forget them?

Carl soon turned out to be the first Canadian painter to render our fields and farmhouses with strong feeling. And this was a region in which I was conscious of following him when I ventured more quietly into pastoral Ontario myself. Another connection, then, between him and me.

Carl Schaefer, 1974
50.8 cm x 61 cm (20" x 24")
Oil on masonite
Collection: Martin Arvenus

27

W.H. Clawson

Will Clawson was a professor of English who specialized in the medieval period and knew his stuff. He was a quiet New Englander, as I like to think can be seen from my portrait of him. If anyone says it reminds him of Grant Wood I should want to clap him on the back.

I was fond of Will in his own silent way. I used to go for a country walk with him every New Year's Day. This was when you could set out from, say, St. Clair Avenue and soon reach open country north of Upper Canada College. My memory tells me that every time we went we saw a king-bird on a telephone wire, but memory can be wrong. If some bird-lover assures me that king-birds go south for the winter, all I can say is that this one didn't.

Such are my happy associations with Will Clawson's portrait. But there is another. A young friend of mine, Glynnis Thomas, was so taken with the picture that she wanted to buy it. My natural impulse was to give it to her, but her father insisted that I let her buy it because it would mean more to her if she paid for it. So I let her do so. She was nineteen years old and paid $150 and has never regretted it.

W.H. Clawson, 1959
40.7 cm x 50.8 cm (16" x 20")
Oil on masonite
Collection: Glynnis Thomas

A.Y. Jackson

Isn't it strange how much in our lives depends on accidents — one accident after another — which, when we look back on them, don't seem like accidents at all, but become part of a continuity. I have never been able to understand this philosophically and have given up trying. What I do know is that if John Hall hadn't said to Alec Jackson, "Come and sit here, Alec, and I'll paint your portrait," I should never have painted mine.

We were putting in a day of heavy rain in a shack on Leech Lake, belonging to our friend Keith MacIver, prior to going up with canoes into the Cloche Mountains to camp in those delectable lakes — Grace Lake, Gem Lake, Little Mountain Lake, and others — for a couple of weeks. Alec dutifully came over with his book and sat down where he was told, and this gave me his reading profile just where I was sitting reading myself. I couldn't resist it. So I immediately got out my paint-box and did him on a sketch-board of 11¼ x 14¼ inches, exactly as you see him now in this reproduction.

We packed up our sketches next morning and forgot all about them until the end of the trip, and then when we started unpacking, there, to our surprise, they were, none the worse for our carrying them all those hundreds of yards uphill and downhill. Alec's only comment on mine, when he saw it, was, "I've got more hair than that." And my reply, "You'll correct that with time." The year was 1940 or thereabouts. It never occurred to me that the portrait would end up in the Art Gallery of Ontario. I don't remember their ever exhibiting it.

By the way, there were six of us on that trip. We all slept in a row crosswise in a big tent with Alec on the outside. When father said turn, we all turned. Wonderful days.

A.Y. Jackson, 1939
28.6 cm x 36.2 cm (11¼" x 14¼")
Oil on wood
Collection: The Art Gallery of Ontario

31

Pegeen Dryer

It would have been hard for me to exclude this portrait. I hesitated briefly for lack of comment. But this had nothing to do with the work. I can succeed just as well with a complete stranger, someone I have never seen before, as with a friend or relative. If anything, the latter may offer more difficulties. Just because. But, in one case as in another, there was always a human face confronting me, and no more was needed. I remember now that Pegeen was first Pegeen Synge and has *The Playboy of the Western World* in her family background.

Pegeen Dryer, 1959
50.8 cm x 61 cm (20" x 24")
Oil on masonite
Private Collection

33

Walter Bauer

Walter Bauer was a German author resident in Toronto. He wrote extensively in his native tongue — verse, biography, autobiography. I feel sure that he wrote daily, almost compulsively. This may not always produce the best results, but it must have been for him part of the act of living. I think of him, now that he is gone, as having existed, as it were, on that plane. This made him a different person, less mundane, less worldly than others, though not less friendly. And this is what ensures that everyone who knew him remembers him and will never forget him.

He was a refugee from Nazi Germany. This is my second key to his character. I don't believe a day passed without his feeling a sense of shame that Hitler spoke the same language as he did. If I wanted companionship in my outlook on the world, I used to drop in on Walter for a chat. He was easy for me to reach because he spent his later years as a member of the German department in my old college. Happily on the whole, I trust. Prior to that he had made a living as best he could, part of the time as a dishwasher, about which experience he afterwards wrote amusingly.

As for the painting, it was a second attempt. I trust it does him justice. But I notice that I came dangerously near to modelling that bald head of his in what is very near to being the conventional way. I had better watch myself.

Walter Bauer, 1956-7
50.8 cm x 61 cm (20" x 24")
Oil on masonite
Private Collection

Charles Meanwell

An added reason I gave myself for including this one of my friend Charles Meanwell in my little gallery of people was that it helped to fill a gap. I felt better provided with men and women of middle age and with children than with young adults. This may only be a hangover from earlier days. Lately, no doubt, I have done something to correct the imbalance, if there was one. Or it may be that my memory simply clings to those I feel nearer to.

It isn't always easy for me to capture the age of my sitters. Mostly, painting as smoothly as I usually do, I get them younger than they are. They never seem to object to this. And if I suggest adding a few wrinkles, they don't encourage me. With Charles, on the other hand, I made him older than he was when I painted him, distinctly older, and it may be a few years more before he catches up with it. I tell him it's up to him now. He has the portrait on his wall and can confer with it whenever he likes. Why shouldn't a portrait have something to say to its subject, especially, perhaps, where there is a difference as well as a similarity? And who knows in the long run whether the difference may prove not to be a difference after all?

Charles Meanwell, 1973
50.8 cm x 61 cm (20" x 24")
Oil on masonite
Collection: Mr. and Mrs. Charles Meanwell

37

James Reaney

James Reaney I regard as a genius with the unique ability to write innocently about things not innocent.

James Reaney, 1958
49.5 cm x 59.7 cm (19½" x 23½")
Oil on masonite
Collection: Mr. and Mrs. Ernest DuVernet

John Pocock

When it comes to saying a word about John Pocock I wish I had known him better. We were on friendly nodding terms for years, but little more than that. For a while he and Nancy worked as silversmiths at the foot of Hazelton Avenue when we were living in a rented apartment at number 16. This was when that area was quiet and on the verge of going downhill. At least the houses on the south side of Yorkville quite close by, where now the Four Seasons Hotel stands, were the slummiest I ever saw in Toronto.

John was very tall, dwarfing all mere six-footers, and grand to behold with that cavernous face in heavy light and shade. "Cavernous" is a risky word to use, but I have to use it. And I had to paint him that way, though I knew he was a Quaker and altogether gentle, as becomes a Quaker. I hope something of this quality in him comes through. Many are the times I told him I wanted him to let me do him, till at last he agreed and gave me a morning or two. Two, I think. And on the second morning when I wanted to complete the figure, having already completed the head, he stood with his arms behind his back just as you see him here. This is my largest portrait, and I shall never have any call to go one bigger.

John Pocock, 1971
81.3 cm x 122 cm (32" x 48")
Oil on masonite
Private Collection

Doris Richardson

Doris and I are friends and painter-friends, dating from the day we met, about a dozen years ago. We both do portraits, and portraits are an endless source of discussion. I have painted her several times and have been slow to choose for this volume. But here is the one I react to excitedly when I come at it again with fresh eyes, as I did the other day. Furthermore, it is the best example I have of my basic style, first clearly shown in the "Jewish Girl" of forty years earlier.

Doris Richardson, 1973
30.5 cm x 40.6 cm (12" x 16")
Oil on masonite
Collection: Doris Richardson

43

Carl Dair

Carl Dair was Canada's leading typographer. There are others, I dare say, equally gifted with him, notably the two MacDonalds, Thoreau and his father, J.E.H. MacDonald. The latter's annual almanac, made for the Arts andLetters Club, and Thoreau's varied work, well illustrated in Edison's volume on him, show that each is a master in this field. The difference is that, unlike the other two, Carl Dair gave his life to it and will have to be so remembered.

According to an authority, Douglas Loughead, the Cartier type-face, which Carl took ten years in designing and finally released at our centenary in 1967, shortly before his death, is "an event of great moment, almost unique in our history." True enough, we pay little attention to lettering and printing and would say off-hand that it is at best a minor art, but the fact remains that we all read print and would no doubt be the better for experiencing its beauty daily in the books and newspapers we read.

Carl Dair, 1963
50.8 cm x 61 cm (20" x 24")
Oil on masonite
Collection: Mr. and Mrs. Peter Dorn

Emil Gartner

It has been said of this portrait of Emil Gartner that it is the best, the strongest thing I ever did. I believe it was an old painter-pal of mine, Aba Bayefsky, who said it to me. And he ought to know after the strong things he has painted himself, in saying which I think chiefly of the darkened faces he did after visiting those prison camps at Belsen and elsewhere. Even without that remark from Aba, I think I should associate my picture of Emil with him as the one that brings me nearer to him than anything else of mine.

Emil was prominent in his day as conductor of the Jewish Folk Choir. Who could forget his conducting in old Massey Hall of *Judas Maccabaeus* and the singing of "Sound the alarm, your silver trumpets sound"? I wish those words could be sung again with loud speakers at street-corners, say once every hour. Would they arouse people to the disregarded world crisis we are living in? I wonder.

If I say these things, which may seem irrelevant to some of you, I can't help it. I haven't seen this portrait lately, but am deeply disturbed by the mere thought of it. Perhaps a painter has no right to get emotionally disturbed at the sight or the thought of one of his own works, let alone proclaim it from the house-tops. But it is true of me in this case and, for better or for worse, I confess it.

Perhaps it is the state of mind I was in when I painted it that upsets me now. Oddly enough, it was made in my room at college, unknown to the authorities. I remember saying to Emil, "You make me think of your grandfather." And what he said to me was, "I don't know anything about my grandfather." And my rejoinder, "It doesn't make any difference." There was that tragic antiquity written all over his face when I contemplated it, just as if he had walked straight out of the desert into Toronto, bringing all the tragedy with him that is part of the Jewish story. When I came to his eyes I said to myself, "Dare I do this?" It seems to me now almost as if I were foreseeing the tragic end Emil himself came to.

Emil Gartner, 1956-7
50.8 cm x 61 cm (20" x 24")
Oil on masonite
Collection: Dr. Alan Powell

Northrop Frye

I first ran into the name of Northrop Frye when, returning to Canada in 1936, I read an article by him in *The Canadian Forum* about that delightful dance troupe "The Ballet Joos." They acted, or rather danced, scenes from social life. I remember particularly "The City," which conveyed both gregariousness and loneliness and gave me a pleasure greater than any I got from classical dancing. Does he remember this too with the same vivid pleasure, I wonder?

He now switches my mind back to the University of Toronto as it was then. It seemed to me in those days that University College with its undenominational freedom was carrying the torch of the humanities ahead of the other colleges. This was a pardonable illusion, which any of the four colleges was entitled to. But what with Northrop Frye and his mastery of the whole field of literature as we know it and his colleague, Kathleen Coburn, with her command of the Coleridge battalion — to say nothing of her very special autobiography *In Pursuit of Coleridge* — it appears now that I was wrong and that Victoria is in the lead as taking the University's name more effectively abroad than I ever expected.

My portrait of Northrop Frye is a third attempt after two ignominious failures. I was with Aba Bayefsky the first time. He succeeded — more than succeeded — and I collapsed. After a second collapse I said, "Norrie, let me try again." He agreed. And sure enough, that inscrutable face of his yielded at last, and his gentle nature came through to my great delight.

Northrop Frye, 1969
61 cm x 76.2 cm (24" x 30")
Oil on masonite
Collection: Professor and Mrs. Northrop Frye

Christopher Grieve

Christopher Grieve was the Scottish poet who published under the name of Hugh MacDiarmid. I painted him twice. Once in Manchester in the mid-thirties, and once much later in Canada. I gave him the first one on his seventieth birthday. He hung it in his favourite pub, Milne's Bar, in Edinburgh, and it was stolen there, it seems, by a member of a football club. Soccer, that is to say. I still like soccer, though. I remember the painting as wild and all-out with his hair blazing vertically at the top and beyond. One of his books has a reproduction of it as a frontispiece. So much for that one.

The second was painted in Toronto in Aba Bayefsky's studio. Christopher had the large one Aba did, and I gave mine — here reproduced — to Christopher's daughter, Christine, then living in Georgetown, Ontario. She promises to do the right thing with it when the right time comes. I am proud of the opportunity he gave me to do him, young and old.

By the way, he was not just a run-of-the-mill poet. On the contrary, I believe him to be the greatest poet of our time writing any kind of English. I say "any kind of English" because he wrote in either difficult Scottish or, sometimes, difficult English. If you want to sample him, read his "Prayer for a Second Flood" and get a Scot to help you. Then read his longer English one "On a Raised Beach." If you don't like either of them, leave him alone.

Hugh MacDiarmid, May 26, 1964
(Christopher Grieve)
40.6 cm x 50.8 cm (16" x 20")
Oil on masonite
Collection: Christine MacIntosh

51

Blodwen Davies

52

In her book on Tom Thomson, Blodwen Davies speaks somewhere of "Canada in her spiritual childhood." And this gives us the key to her whole life and occupation. She was initially a journalist, and as time went by, a writer of books, all of them, to the best of my knowledge, devoted to her native country, its outward scene, its culture, its future. Titles like *The Saguenay* and *Paddle and Palette* speak for themselves.

It was appropriate that she should write the first book on Thomson. Looking back, it seems strange that we had to wait nearly twenty years for it. And even then in 1935 it had to be privately printed and privately circulated. Publication proper came later still in 1967, the year after Blodwen's death, and fifty years after Tom Thomson's. All of this goes to show what a pioneer Blodwen was in her thought about her country. I used to visit her in her later years at Markham and shall always bear her happily in mind. As do all others who know her. A good Canadian. More need not be said.

Blodwen Davies, 1960
40.6 cm x 50.8 cm (16" x 20")
Oil on masonite
Private Collection

53

Huntly Gordon

Huntly Gordon was the closest friend my family had. This makes him hard to write about. The remarkable thing was that in spite of the haemophilia that he fought against for nearly sixty years, as an invalid or semi-invalid, he was by nature an outdoorsman and man of action. The consequence is that when I look back on him in the long ago, my mind jumps to two things in the world of nature — to wild birds and canoeing.

First, then, he taught me how to paddle a canoe with what he said was the Ojibway stroke, propelling and steering all in one movement. This stood me in good stead on the many canoe trips I took in Georgian Bay, Algonquin Park and Timmagami. If anything made me feel Canadian it was my canoe.

And then birds — the various thrushes, the two loon calls, and all the rest. Most of it is forgotten now, especially as there are so few birds about in the city. Gone now are the days when I saw a cardinal in my backyard on Willcocks Street or took my students to the window in University College to see a flock of blue-birds in the Dean's garden. It wasn't till I came to Canada that I began to observe, thanks to Huntly most of all.

Huntly Gordon, 1937
30.5 cm x 40.6 cm (12" x 16")
Oil on canvas
Collection: Mrs. and Mrs. Ezra Schabas

John Hall

John Hall and me. That could be a rich story. He gave me four — I believe reasonably happy — granddaughters. But this isn't the place to say it, so I had better stop and start again.

We met in 1936, when I came back to Toronto, and we soon went sketching together in that lovely country north of Palgrave, backed by the Dingle, my favourite bit of pastoral Ontario. John has encouraged me as a painter ever since. He made slides of my heads and landscapes which he shows again and again, not only at the School of Architecture, where he belongs, but all over the place. He has the gift to draw people out and make them find themselves as artists, sometimes I think at the expense of his own time and work. My indebtedness to him over the years is immense.

This study of him was prompted by his posture. Seeing him sitting that way I said, "John, I could paint you like that." And I did and think it very characteristic.

John Hall, c. 1938
76.2 cm x 101.6 cm (30" x 40")
Oil on masonite
Private Collection

Joan Hall

There are four paintings in all of my daughter Joan, two of them done when we were living in England, 1932-36, both quite small, one of them a simple profile in green, barely characterized, and the other, the earlier of the two, wild-eyed and exciting and possibly what some would say I should have chosen instead of the one you see.

But this — the third of the four — is by all odds the portrait I can't help thinking she would have preferred herself. It was done at 10 Kilbarry Road not long after our return to Canada, but not before she had become Joan Hall. I remember the three of us sitting there, John looking on as I painted — the only time I ever allowed anyone to watch me at work — and the portrait coming along without a pause or hitch until suddenly it was there. Why sometimes a picture paints itself, as it were, effortlessly and another is a slow struggle, yet when the two are put side by side you can't say which is which, is another of painting's mysteries, not requiring an answer, though intriguing to ask.

Joan Hall, 1938
50.8 cm x 61 cm (20" x 24")
Oil on canvas
Collection: Mr. and Mrs. John Hall

Vincent Thomas

It so happens that I was Vince's first visitor at Jackknife, a lodge with cottages, which he had built more or less with his own hands on the outer shore of Georgian Bay, north of Parry Sound. From that time on my family and friends frequently holidayed there.

The memorable day was when John Hall came over to me and said, "We are going to paint Vince at the shack. Will you come over and paint him with us?" Somehow or other I had stopped painting some years before and had no thought of ever painting again. So I resisted his proposal. But I finally yielded to pressure. They sat me down and gave me some paints and a couple of brushes and a board of masonite, and I painted this portrait rapidly.

For me it was the great resumption. I have painted steadily ever since, that is to say from about 1953 on. Most of what you see in this book belongs to these years.

Head, 1953
(Vincent Thomas)
50.8 cm x 40.6 cm (20" x 16")
Oil on masonite
Collection: Mr. and Mrs. Vincent Thomas

61

Becky Hall

This of my granddaughter Becky — now Becky Proctor — was also done at Jackknife, a day or two later than Vince. I was still reluctant to start, but I was told that Becky wanted it. So I agreed to try, or rather pretend to try, with the firm intention of pulling out at the first opportunity, when suddenly Becky, finding herself bored after thinking it would be fun, slumped into this despairing posture with her hands behind her head. I found her irresistible and lost no time in getting it recorded.

Becky (Unwilling Sitter), 1953
39.4 cm x 27.9 cm (15½" x 11")
Oil on wood
Collection: Mr. and Mrs. Phillip Proctor

E.J. Pratt

When I first started to paint portraits, having no experience and even less reputation, I sometimes innocently gave them to the sitters without asking whether they wanted them. This was a mistake. I can remember at least four cases where the portraits disappeared or were got rid of.

Ned Pratt's is the worst case of all. I gave him this little head and more or less forgot about it myself, till years later it came back into my mind as possibly worth recovering and I succeeded in doing so. An old friend of Ned's at Longbranch had it, I was told. John Hall and I went out to see it and we both held our breath at the sight of it, because Ned was so clearly there. The owner in her generosity said she thought it ought to come back to me. So off we went with it gleefully. It had been badly scraped and I had to repaint two patches in the face. I managed to do this so successfully that I couldn't tell you where the patches were. Northrop Frye now has it. It seems to me truer to Ned Pratt than that official big one where he looks like a member of the upper class, which he certainly wasn't. You can tell that from his verse even if you hadn't the good fortune to know him in person. He was a joy to know.

There is no reason why I should talk about his verse here. Neither is there any reason why I shouldn't. I always believed that as a Canadian poet he was on sounder lines than any, seeing that he never stewed in his juice but looked out from himself at great events in our record. He was the one poet we have who might have written the Canadian epic that Canada calls for — look only at our geography — especially at a time when the unity of Canada is threatened and its break-up not beyond the bounds of possibility. How wonderful it would be to have a Canadian poem that might stand beside Charles M. Doughty's "The Dawn in Britain," which George Bernard Shaw said should be reprinted and made available to schoolboys as an introduction to their country's beginnings, or beside "John Brown's Body," which is the nearest we have yet come to an epic of North America. This may be an idle dream, but if Ned were here, I am sure he would approve.

E.J. Pratt, 1939
28.6 cm x 39.4 cm (11¼" x 15½")
Oil on wood panel
Collection: Professor and Mrs. Northrop Frye

Hugh Garner

Not having any longer good eyesight for extended reading, I can't claim to have read everything Hugh Garner wrote, the less so as they now put him into such small print. But I have read *Cabbagetown* and a number of shorter things, one of which stays so persistently in my mind that it dominates my recollection of him. It sticks in my head like Maupassant's necklace.

I read it in *The Tamarack Review* not many years ago. A man driving alone in the North American West picked up a couple who signalled him, a man and a lame girl, and took them along. The three of them stayed overnight at the same place, and in his kindness, he took them on again next morning. Suddenly the man attacked or threatened the driver dangerously, and what did the girl do? She smashed his skull in from behind with a crutch or a stick and put him permanently out of business. The other two, left with his corpse, disposed of it unseen in that waste country and then agreed to part company without exchanging names. That's all. The tale is quite complete, yet it invites the reader to extend it forward and backward in time beyond its printed limits.

I asked Hugh Garner whether he planned the girl's conduct from the beginning. And he said no; it came to him, so to speak, when it happened. Spontaneously then, just as it must have come spontaneously to her. This must be why it works so memorably. Remember, by the way, that she was lame.

What I will claim for my portrait of him is that it is not unlike this story, and therefore justifies my brief telling of it here. We only met that once, on the day I painted him.

Hugh Garner, 1975
40.6 cm x 50.8 cm (16" x 20")
Oil on masonite
Private Collection

67

Zalman Yanofsky

Here is the Zal who was later the leader of a rock group, very popular in the sixties, with the name of "The Lovin' Spoonful," and who, by contrast, is now running a restaurant in Kingston, Ontario, called "Chez Piggy." So I am told.

Little, if anything, of this spicy reason is anticipated in the portrait of him, painted in 1962 when he was in his teens or barely out of them. Not that it matters now, I say to myself. Nor does it matter whether or not my personal view of humanity has crept into my viewing of him, as it is bound to have done pervasively in all my work without my knowing anything about it. Anyway schoolboys are not easy to capture. I like to think that I have succeeded here.

Would you believe it, that the blues in this picture have no blue paint in them? They are simply raw umber and white. The adjacent warm colours give them their blueness. This sort of thing happens all the time, if you keep to a restricted palette, as I do.

Zalman Yanofsky, 1962
39.4 cm x 50.8 cm (15½" x 20")
Oil on masonite
Private Collection

69

Robertson Davies

It stands to reason that a portrait painter of my sort when confronted with Robertson Davies asks himself whether he can pull it off in this case without compromising himself. "Can I manage to set down so well-known a countenance and stay true to myself in doing so? Committed as I am — and have been from the word go — to relying on lines and flat areas without any orthodox modelling, can I set him down so that people at large will say, 'This is he'?"

Having got on the cover of *The Canadian Forum* with him, I believe I can rest assured. And I certainly made no compromise. My bold treatment of the left eye and brow above it came naturally and easily to me and served my purpose. So I can breathe freely. Looking at the portrait now, I can see that I somewhat emphasized the vertical, but this came of itself unintentionally. I often find that in painting portraits I am in complete control at the start, but sooner or later the half-finished work starts dictating to me, and I have to listen to it. With a different board I might have done differently.

I was told afterwards that the yellow of the background accorded with the magical element in *Fifth Business*. All I can say in reply is that this never remotely occurred to me. It will be clear to anyone who knows my work that I regularly prefer a restricted palette based on earth colours, which means that I prefer yellows to reds and blues. I just drifted slowly into using yellow here without any thought or theory in doing so.

Robertson Davies, 1973
76.2 cm x 101.6 cm (30" x 40")
Oil on masonite
Collection: Alan Walker

George Johnston

"Mr. Murple's got a dog that's long
And underslung and sort of pointed wrong."

These are the opening lines of "Noctambule," a George Johnston poem that I have a sneaking relish for. You will find it in his first book of verse, *The Cruising Auk* (Oxford 1951).

Whoever turns the pages of this little volume will find such a variety of mood, ranging from high spirits to low, and so full of surprises as to leave him in no doubt that George Johnston is not a simple person who can easily be put in a nutshell. How, then, could a painter hope to put the whole of him into a single portrait — least of all myself who never claims to capture more than a single aspect of a sitter and am content if I capture that much? If I do two or three studies of the same person I may get a different aspect each time, but I seldom feel, even then, that I am reaching or approaching the portrayal of the whole person. In saying this I am not apologetic. I think it much more satisfactory to bring to life one aspect of a person than to provide mere recognition, which may enable you to say, "This is John Smith," without telling you any more about John Smith than you knew before. Official portraits seldom do better than this.

What, for me, distinguished George from other many-sided people is that there isn't any aspect of him that I am out of tune with. Consequently, when we meet, which is only occasionally, I am apt to gossip with him without keeping my eye on the clock. The morning I painted him — I often complete a portrait in the course of a morning — we gossiped away until it was almost too late to finish, and I suddenly blurted out, "George, it's time we stopped talking and painted." This may have been at about half-past eleven. I piled in then and completed my portrait before lunch. No doubt it bears the marks of speed, but it may be for this very reason that it brings George Johnston to life.

George Johnston, c. 1955
40.7 cm x 50.8 cm (16" x 20")
Oil on masonite
Collection: Professor and Mrs. Claude Bissell

Eddie Providence

Not having talked much with Eddie Providence, I can't say more about him than that he is a student of music and a writer of music and as friendly a fellow as I have ever met. If this latter fails to come out in the portrait I did of him, it is the portrait's fault. Some would say it is my fault. But I am not sure. Portraits have a way with them.

From my point of view, he was a welcome subject and I made the most of him. I deliberately chose a green underpainting, hoping that it would work with his complexion. And work I believe it did. It had always been my practice to paint on white or off-white, but as time went by, I found myself drifting into colour. How I so drifted is amusing. I invariably clean my palette at the end of each painting, and after a while, I got into the habit of mixing up the leftover paint and rubbing it into a new board, so as not to waste it. Parsimony, you see, brings its rewards. This may be the first time I prepared a specific colour for a specific sitter. I have done the same with a strong yellow and a strong blue, as will be seen elsewhere on these pages. But my better judgement tells me that I mustn't abuse this attractive device.

Eddie Providence, 1973
75.6 cm x 101.6 cm (29¾" x 40")
Oil on masonite
Private Collection

Brigitte

I can't remember this little German girl's name or anything definite about her, though, if I set about it, I could reconstruct her. But it would be of no interest to anyone and nothing would be gained. So I will leave it at Brigitte, presumably Bridget in our tongue, but here pronounced hard in three syllables, like combining the sound of "brig" and the sound of "gitter," if there were such a word.

There is an unforced pathos in this face, which came of itself, not planned or foreseen. Everyone feels it.

Brigitte, 1959
40.6 cm x 50.8 cm (16" x 20")
Oil on masonite
Collection: Mr. and Mrs. Vincent Thomas

BARKER FAIRLEY

77

Karl Rix

Karl Rix is a friend I feel of as lost. Not just because he now lives in East Berlin, but because, as his wife Lauretta assured me, he never on any account writes a letter. The two of them lived here for years with their two daughters, he from Vienna and she from Montreal, and never managed to make an easy living as artists, gifted as they both were. Karl may be doing better where he is, working at times in a team. Alone he was apt to labour a picture like the wonderful one of me he did from behind, a back view, and then spoiled. I, in my turn, painted them one after another, and they took the four boards away with them. Also, I did them all together on one big board, which was not good enough to show, but good enough for me to keep and remember them by. As for this of him, I know it is not unlike him. I only hope that his native gentleness shows through the rugged exterior.

Karl Rix, 1963
50.8 cm x 61 cm (20" x 24")
Oil on masonite
Private Collection

Eugène Vinaver

If you pushed me into the corner and made me choose the portrait I like best in this selection, I might have to choose this one of Eugène Vinaver. Not on personal grounds, though on that score I know he would run everybody close, but for a painter's reason. This portrait impresses me as being the best of the lot because it combines my style at its most uncompromising with a characterization at its fullest.

By good luck I hit on an underpainting, no doubt previously made and lying around waiting to be used, which suited my purpose, so that, as with Donald Creighton, I only painted the face and left the rest undeveloped. This lets the face stand out much more vividly than if I had fussed over the shoulders and the background, which seem to me to serve the purpose just as they are.

Since literary scholars are seldom in the public eye, I might add that Eugène is outstanding in the fields of French and English and was in great demand as a visiting lecturer. This brought him not long ago to Toronto and enabled us to meet again after many, many years and be happy together. It was in Manchester in the thirties that we first met. His best-known contribution to English letters is his three-volume edition of Malory, based on the so-called Winchester manuscript, which he discovered. John Steinbeck retold the story of King Arthur in the light of it.

Eugène Vinaver, 1976
40.6 cm x 50.8 cm (16" x 20")
Oil on masonite
Private Collection

FAIRLEY

81

Louisa

Louisa is Louisa Schabas, a great-granddaughter at the age of three. This is as far back as I have been able to go.

The amazing thing to me is that I have succeeded with little ones at all, because, as my own children could tell you, I wasn't good with them and preferred to wait benevolently for them to get a little older rather than adapt myself to the infant mind. Yet I must have managed to paint them before I could entertain them, because I remember having an exhibition of children only, some twenty of them, at the School of Architecture. As I can't lay hands on more than one or two of these portraits now, their parents must have liked them well enough to procure them. Possibly more with a view to the future than to the present. But no matter.

There is no sense in expecting a child to sit for you. Your only hope is to make a quick decision and record it at once for better or for worse. At most you can say, "Run away now and come back when you want." My experience is that they invariably come trotting back again, quickly, at least once, whereas adults are apt to stray into chatting with someone and leaving you stuck. With Louisa those little dark eyes were all I needed, along with a minimum of everything else, to get a living face.

Louisa Schabas, 1980
30.5 cm x 40.6 cm (12" x 16")
Oil on masonite
Private Collection

FAIRLEY

Dick Schabas

This is the last of the children to get selected for the book. Why it wasn't the first I can't imagine. In the Schabas family's set of five, hanging on their walls, Ann and Ezra by a narrow margin put it just ahead of the others. By virtue, I suspect, of the special look it has of being surprised or of questioning, as if to say, "What's going on now?" Dick, by the way, is now a medical practitioner, asking questions of another sort.

Dick Schabas, c. 1956
28 cm x 35.6 cm (11" x 14")
Oil on masonite
Collection: Dr. Richard Schabas

Mary Simmons

It was at a Schabas party that I met Mary Simmons. She showed interest in some of my portraits of grandchildren which she caught sight of on the walls. And this led to my painting her portrait. It is natural to prefer sitters who are interested in your work, or at least not indifferent to it.

Although she is a dramatic soprano, I somehow, when I started the portrait, shifted her in my mind from music to literature, where I am better versed, and thought of her as an actress in a Racine play. Think of *Athalie*. This, I believe, is what gives the portrait its special quality, or rather heightens its special quality in the direction of the heroic and tragic.

This was an unusual thing for me to do. My usual argument, when questioned about a sitter's character, is to maintain that I gave no thought to it in the act of painting but simply worked visually as if the face before me were a landscape for me to find my own terms for, emphasizing this and ignoring that, all with a view to making it click, as it were, and with a chief concern with composition, colour, texture. No doubt the two personalities confronting one another are involved all the time — how could it be otherwise — but involved only in the sense that the involvement looks after itself, not in the sense that it needs to be watched. Without the idea of Racine I might have arrived at a somewhat different study of Mary, perhaps more friendly and domestic, but I don't for a moment regret the result I got.

The colours I used here have often intrigued me since. Exclusively black and white and green except for the lips; cold colours I would have thought them, yet the picture doesn't affect me, or anyone else, as cold. But I have never used these colours predominantly again.

Mary Simmons, 1965
50.8 cm x 61 cm (20" x 24")
Oil on masonite
Private Collection

87

Leopold Infeld

It is sad that Leopold Infeld is so little remembered in Canada apart from a handful of mathematicians and a handful of friends. He was one of the notable people driven across the Atlantic by a disturbed Europe in the nineteen-thirties. In his case, out of his native Poland by a devious journey — publishing with and writing about Einstein en route — into Canada, where he stayed for twelve years as a member of the University of Toronto staff.

Political mutterings against him led to his deciding to return to Poland in 1950. He told me himself that if the University had spoken on his behalf he would have stayed on here. Perhaps for life. Sam Beatty, head of his department, said to me later, "I don't think we were very kind to Infeld," whereupon I whispered to myself, "Yes, but you waited a long time to say it."

It seems, however, that Leopold did well to go home again, professionally. His native country welcomed him back and made him head of the Institute of Theoretical Physics in Warsaw. He had eighteen more years of productive life. He died in 1968.

One of the things he did while in Canada was to write an autobiography, *Quest,* which I would very much like to see reprinted. Gilbert Robinson has said that Infeld's life was "in microcosm the life of our century," and this is reflected in his book. It was written in Canada by one who resided in Canada. I don't see why it can't be kept alive as a piece of Canadian literature. There is nowhere else for it to go.*

As for my portrait of him, I will only say that Leopold had a rich vein of fun in him as well as a deep seriousness. I trust that both of these characteristics are reflected here.

* Since my writing the above, *Quest* has been republished.

Leopold Infeld, c. 1937
40.6 cm x 50.8 cm (16" x 20")
Oil on canvas
Collection: Professor and Mrs. Viljo Packer

John Sommer

What shall I say about John Sommer? I am happy to have made a portrait of him that I can include because I owe so much to him. Perhaps a miniature biography will serve.

He came from North Germany to Canada hoping to farm, and ended up in Georgetown working in a welding factory. Being devoted to art and finding on trial that he wasn't, by his own standards, cut out to be an artist, he decided to help others. For fifteen years he has held exhibitions in his house in that lovely older part of Georgetown — Gallery House Sol, 35 Charles Street — guided throughout by his love of art, without ever making concessions to the thought of money-making. Simply showing the works of artists he approved of whether they sold or not. He is now running smooth, he tells me, after many difficult years.

How he managed in his spare time to get through the physical task of putting on a show is little short of a mystery. But it will be apparent from my portrait of him, with his right arm grasping the back of the chair he was sitting in as if he couldn't stay seated any longer — a position he dropped into after I had started — that he is a man of immense energy and enthusiasm. If I had anything to do with the awarding of medals, civic, provincial or national, I would see that he got one. Meanwhile, all power to him.

John Sommer, 1970
75.6 cm x 101.6 cm (29¾" x 40")
Oil on masonite
Collection: Mr. and Mrs. John Sommer

Henry Beissel

Among the cluster of young Germans who came to Canada in the mid-century and contributed so richly to our life, Henry Beissel stands out. Think of a non-English speaker — born in Cologne in 1929 — coming to Canada in his twenties, mastering the language, and exploring not only our cities but also — the most remarkable thing we have — our geography and giving us an extraordinary Eskimo play, *Inook and the Sun,* in which a young Eskimo boy strives to capture the sun and bring it back for all the year round and, in so striving, sets the elements talking together. Every Canadian, child or adult, ought to know this work. Has it been prescribed for school reading? If not, why not? Henry wrote much else besides, but in this context I needn't dilate. Remember *Inook.*

Henry Beissel, c. 1965
40.6 cm x 50.8 cm (16" x 20")
Oil on masonite
Collection: Professor and Mrs. Henry Beissel

93

Herbert Whittaker

Herbert Whittaker is our gentleman in the field of literary and dramatic criticism, and I like this quality in him. If I may compare notes, I can say that I never wrote about authors and painters I didn't care about, though I recognize that polemical critics like Nathan Cohen have their place and serve their purpose. In private life Herbert is just the same as in public, and we were happy together. I hope he approves of the portrait.

Herbert Whittaker, 1972
60.3 cm x 76 cm (23¾" x 30")
Oil on masonite
Collection: Mr. and Mrs. Ernest DuVernet

Paul Sweetman

This study of Paul I have always felt especially proud of without asking myself why. I painted it years ago and have looked at it frequently since, but only now do I begin to see the light. I remember saying suddenly to myself that if a familiar friend of Paul's were walking up to the picture, he would say that this was Paul long before he was near enough to identify the features, because in a very special way the whole thing is Paul and not just the face.

Have I, for once, pulled off what you might call a visually total portrait as against merely a true facial likeness? A portrait, that is, in which the sitter's person permeates the whole, is reflected in the whole? I believe I have. I may never repeat the experience, but I shall always hang on to the idea and am grateful to Paul for putting it into my head.

If I were writing biographies here, Paul would score, being capable of staging Gilbert and Sullivan operettas one day and digging up an Indian village the day after.

Paul Sweetman, 1957
40.6 cm x 50.8 cm (16" x 20")
Oil on masonite
Collection: Mr. and Mrs. Paul Sweetman

Nan Fairley

It isn't easy for me to comment on Nan because we joined forces some ten years ago when I was left living alone and I am, as it were, prejudiced. She has kept me alive daily since we met and proposes to continue doing so while we both exist. It followed of itself that I painted portraits of her repeatedly, some coming close to her, others even distant, yet worth preserving as bearing on humanity. For inclusion here I have chosen this white-on-yellow one, both as being the most recent and as being, by a narrow margin, the pick of them. There are at least three others that run it close. This one came easily on a yellow ground which shows through everywhere, all over the dress, and even between the lips and between the fingers. At the finish I slightly deepened the yellow of the background.

Nan seems to me an interesting case in relation to visual art. When we met and I first showed her my work, she simply said she didn't understand it. Then — a day or two later, not more — she looked at it again and said she did understand it. And, believe it or not, she was completely abreast of modern art from then on in all its phases, Picasso, Chagall, or anyone else you like to name. To the best of my knowledge, she had never, though widely read in great literature, given a thought to the visual arts. And here, almost overnight, she was completely at home in them. She is the person I enjoy consulting when in the middle of one of my things, and I invariably profit.

Nan Fairley, 1977
61 cm x 101.6 cm (24" x 40")
Oil on masonite
Collection: Nan Fairley

Laura Hofrichter

Laura Hofrichter was the first person to talk to me about my portraits as a whole and about their human meaning. The thought has been in my mind ever since. I came to the conclusion recently that if I had worked more conventionally there would be less to say. But, as they stand, there is clearly an outlook on life in them that must have come from me, though I never gave it a thought while painting. What that outlook is I can't easily say, and there is no need for me to try. It can be left to the observer to reach his own conclusions.

Laura Hofrichter, 1958-9
50.8 cm x 61 cm (20" x 24")
Oil on masonite
Private Collection

"Was willst du, dass von deiner Gesinnung
    man dir nach ins Ewige sende?"
"Er gehörte zu keiner Innung,
    Blieb Liebhaber bis ans Ende."

                                    — GOETHE

• LIST OF PLATES •

• SELECTED BIBLIOGRAPHY •

Books by Barker Fairley

Charles M. Doughty. London: Jonathan Cape, 1927.

Goethe As Revealed In His Poetry. London: J.M. Dent, 1932.

A Study of Goethe. Oxford: Clarendon Press, 1947.

Goethe's Faust: Six Essays. Oxford: Clarendon Press, 1953

Heinrich Heine: An Interpretation. Oxford: Clarendon Press, 1954. German translation by Laura Hofrichter, 1965.

Georgian Bay Sketches. Toronto: University of Toronto Press, 1957.

Wilhelm Raabe. Oxford: Clarendon Press, 1961. German translation, Munich 1961.

Poems of 1922 Or Not Long After. Kingston: H. Heine Press, 1972.

Poems by Barker Fairley. Toronto: Yonge Street Press, 1977.

Edited by Barker Fairley

Gottfried Keller. *Der Grüne Heinrich.* Oxford: Clarendon Press, 1925.

Selected Passages from The Dawn in Britain (by Charles M. Doughty). London: Duckworth, 1935.

Goethe. *Selected Letters.* Oxford: Blackwell, 1955.

Selected Poems of Goethe. London: Heinemann, 1965.

Heinrich Heine. *Selected Poems.* Don Mills: Heine Press, 1965.

Heinrich Heine. *Atta Troll* and *Deutschland.* London: Oxford University Press, 1966.

Translated by Barker Fairley

Goethe's Faust. Toronto: University of Toronto Press, 1972.

Colour photography (except page 31) by
Hans Geerling Photography Ltd., Toronto.

Colour photograph of A.Y. Jackson, page 31,
supplied by the Art Gallery of Ontario.

Photograph page ii
courtesy of Reg Innell.

Colour separations by
Graphic Litho-Plate Inc., Toronto.

Phototypesetting by The Carswell Printing
Company Limited.

Printed on 200 M Imperial Offset Enamel
and bound in Bayside Linen by The Carswell
Printing Company Limited.